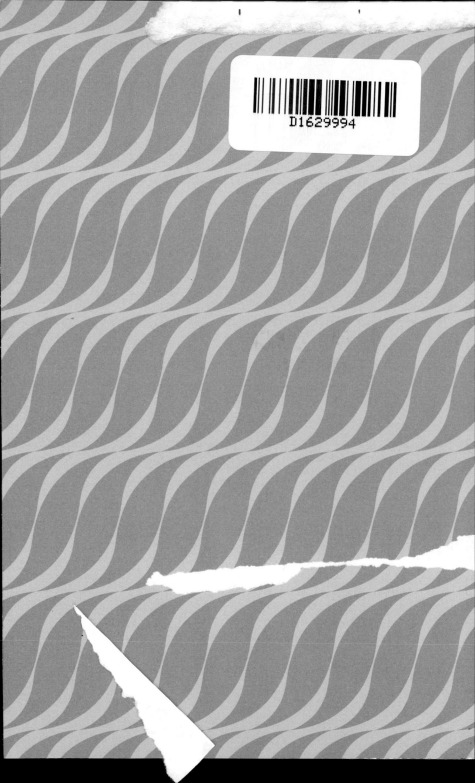

D1629994

GREAT SANDWICHES

Consultant Editor:
Valerie Ferguson

southwater

Contents

Introduction

Whether you are looking for a substantial snack for lunch, a perfect after-school munch, a hospitable greeting to unexpected visitors, a tasty party morsel and a quick-and-easy, nourishing treat for whatever time of day you feel hungry, there is a sandwich that fits the bill. The recipes in this book include Classics, from traditional English tea-time triangles of wafer-thin bread to robust American specialities bursting with fillings and flavour. Hot Sandwiches offer a melt-in-the-mouth collection of substantial snacks for cold days, while Hearty Sandwiches, filled with eggs, cheese, chicken or salami, are a meal in themselves. Children's Sandwiches features intriguing ways of serving choosy little people with tasty and nourishing food that they will find irresistible. Finally, Open & Party Sandwiches is packed with recipes for easy, yet elegant entertaining.

The book provides practical information about the many excellent breads that are now widely available and the ingredients that make superb fillings. It even guides you through elegant garnishes and planning and preparation, so that you can make the world's most popular snack a great sandwich every time.

Breads

Interesting breads, available in different sizes, shapes, textures, flavours and colours, allow the sandwich enthusiast to produce some exciting creations.

White Bread

Forget pre-packaged, pre-sliced bread. Bakeries and many supermarkets produce their own varieties, full of flavour and with a good texture. Crusty cottage loaves are good for toasted and hearty sandwiches.

White bread

Wholemeal Bread

Many people prefer wholemeal bread because of its flavour and texture. A slice of wholemeal can be combined with a slice of white bread for a *Wholemeal bread* chequerboard sandwich. Granary bread is a multi-grain bread with a lighter, crunchier texture than wholemeal.

Rye Bread

Both light and dark rye breads are available. They are especially delicious with smoked fish or pickled herring. Pumpernickel is a heavy, close-textured black rye bread which is cut very thinly and makes an excellent base for open sandwiches with strongly flavoured toppings. Rye with sunflower seeds is similar to pumpernickel, but lighter in colour.

Dark rye bread

Continental Breads

Best known are baguettes or French sticks. These can be cut *Baguette* lengthways, grilled and cut into lengths that suit the appetite. Also from France, brioche is a light, rich, slightly sweet bread that, when toasted, makes a good base for open sandwiches. A light-textured, Italian bread, made with olive oil, ciabatta is available both plain and flavoured. Pugliese, also known as Italian peasant bread, is a close-textured loaf made with olive oil.

Rolls & Individual Breads

Bagels, the basis of many American recipes, are best served warm and are especially good filled with cream cheese and smoked salmon or mackerel pâté. Pitta *Bagels* breads are available in both wholemeal and white and in rounds, ovals and mini-cocktail shapes. Baps are large, soft rolls, sometimes with a seed *Croissants* topping. They are especially good with a hearty, hot filling. Croissants are delicious with both sweet and savoury fillings. Warm them first, then split and fill.

Filling Ingredients

There is a huge variety of sandwich ingredients to use individually or in interesting and unusual combinations.

Dairy

Choose strongly flavoured cheeses, such as blue cheese, to combine with fruit, and blend creamy Brie with avocado. For melting, use Gruyère, Emmenthal and Mozzarella which have the best texture.

Gruyère cheese

Eggs are versatile and can be used in a variety of fillings. For a luxurious touch, use tiny speckled quail's eggs but cook them for only 3 minutes.

Quail's eggs

For spreading, you can beat herbs or other flavourings into softened, unsalted butter. Parsley, lemon rind, tarragon and anchovy essence will all transform its flavour.

Fish & Seafood

Prawns go well with a variety of mayonnaise-based dressings. Fresh, North Atlantic prawns have the best flavour. Frozen prawns must be completely defrosted and thoroughly dried with kitchen paper before using. Rollmops and other varieties of pickled herring are excellent for open sandwiches. Smoked salmon is ideal for open sandwiches, and other smoked fish, especially mackerel, are also suitable.

Prawns

Meat

Use thinly sliced Parma ham for delicate party sandwiches, or rare roast beef, good-quality hams and smoked or unsmoked salamis for tasty lunches. Pastrami is cured, smoked brisket of beef; it is best served with a strong-flavoured bread.

Vegetables

Cucumber, tomatoes and lettuce are sandwich classics. Other useful salad vegetables include radicchio, frisée, rocket, chicory and crunchy peppers.

Tomatoes

Herbs & Flavourings

Fresh herbs give a terrific zip to sandwich fillings. Use basil with tomatoes, fennel and dill with fish, marjoram and oregano with eggs.

Basil

Lemon is a tasty addition to fish fillings, and olives are excellent on toasted toppings. Use mustards to hot up meats – medium-hot Dijon, grainy Meaux or sweet-sour German mustard are all worth exploring. Enliven fillings with basil or sun-dried tomato pesto, or use black olive paste or tapenade instead of butter.

Mustards

Planning & Preparing

While making a quick sandwich is one of the easiest kitchen tasks,
preparing attractive and appetizing ones requires a little more thought.

It is essential to consider how many
people will be eating and how much time
there will be for preparation. Some of the
work can be done in advance – although
it is rarely wise to assemble sandwiches
completely beforehand. Don't plan too
many hot snacks if you are throwing a
party, or you will spend the whole
evening in the kitchen. A choice of
vegetarian and non-vegetarian fillings is
thoughtful for a social gathering.

Have a good supply of different breads,
filling ingredients and garnishes, but do
not slice the bread too far in advance.
Many garnishes, however, have to be
prepared in advance and left to curl in
iced water. Mayonnaise and most other
dressings can also be prepared, covered
with clear film and kept in the fridge.
Many ingredients can also be prepared

earlier – grate cheese and keep it in a
covered container in the fridge, wash salad
leaves and herbs, pat dry and store in
sealed plastic bags in the fridge. Anything
that needs to be cooked and cooled

should be prepared in good time. Fillings
that are combined with a dressing, can
usually be prepared and stored in the
fridge. However, do not make anything
containing avocado or apple in advance or
it will discolour. Remove butter from the
fridge for it to soften.

Making Sandwiches

Have all the ingredients ready before you
start and, if preparing hot sandwiches,
preheat the grill or oven. Make sure knives
are sharp – both bread and many filling
ingredients often need to be thinly sliced.

If removing crusts, it is often easier to
spread the butter, mayonnaise or tapenade
beforehand to ensure that the slice is fully
covered. Some sandwiches are best
assembled before cutting off the crusts
and then cutting them into quarters.

Fillings should always be generous but
sandwiches should not be so packed that
they disintegrate while being eaten.

Always garnish sandwiches – however
simply – as they look more appetizing.

Garnishes

Adding a garnish to sandwiches not only looks good but also adds to the flavour. Here are some creative suggestions.

Radish Rose

Remove the stalk, and with the pointed end of a vegetable knife cut petal shapes around the bottom half of the radish, keeping them joined at the base. Cut a second 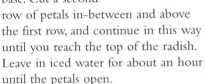 row of petals in-between and above the first row, and continue in this way until you reach the top of the radish. Leave in iced water for about an hour until the petals open.

Cucumber Butterflies

Cut a 1 cm/½ in length of cucumber and halve lengthways into 2 semicircles. Cut each into 7 slices, leaving them attached along one edge. Fold every other slice back on itself to form the butterfly.

Carrot Curl

Using a potato peeler, remove thin strips of carrot. Roll each strip to make a curl and secure in place with a cocktail stick. Place the carrot curls in iced water for about an hour to keep the shape. Drain on kitchen paper.

Spring Onion Tassel

Trim a spring onion to about 7.5 cm/3 in long. Cut lengthways through the green part of the onion several times, to within 4 cm/1½ in of the white end. Place in a bowl of cold water for about an hour, until the ends curl up.

Radish Chrysanthemum

First remove the stalk, then cut downwards across the radish, using a sharp knife, at 2 mm/1/16 in intervals, keeping the radish joined at the base. Then cut in the opposite direction to form minute squares. Drop the radish chrysanthemum into iced water for about an hour, until it opens out like a flower.

Tomato Rose

Choose a firm tomato and, starting at the smooth end, pare off the skin in a continuous strip about 1 cm/½ in wide using a very sharp knife. With the flesh-side inwards, start to curl the strip of skin from the base end, forming a bud shape. Continue winding the strip until it forms a flower. Place carefully on to the food for garnishing.

Mayonnaise & Simple Fillings

Mouthwatering sandwich fillings or toppings can be quickly and simply made using these basic recipes.

Mayonnaise

Ready-made mayonnaise works well for sandwiches, but there is more depth of flavour and a creamier texture to the home-made variety.

Makes about 350 ml/
12 fl oz/1½ cups

INGREDIENTS
2 egg yolks
2.5 ml/½ tsp Dijon mustard
300 ml/½ pint/1¼ cups sunflower oil
10 ml/2 tsp wine vinegar
salt and freshly ground black pepper

1 Beat the egg yolks, seasoning and mustard together in a bowl with a hand whisk. Add the oil drop by drop, whisking vigorously.

2 As the mixture thickens, add the vinegar, then continue to add the remaining oil in a steady stream, whisking all the time. Add a little boiling water to thin, if necessary.

Avocado Filling

This filling is particularly suitable for sandwich horns or on open sandwiches.

Fills 3 rounds sandwiches

INGREDIENTS
1 avocado, stoned and chopped
1 spring onion, chopped
10 ml/2 tsp lemon juice
dash of Worcestershire sauce
salt and freshly ground black pepper

Put the avocado pieces in a blender, or mash with a fork until smooth. Mix in the chopped spring onion, lemon juice and seasonings and blend well.

Tuna & Tomato Filling

A useful filling that can be made using store-cupboard ingredients. It is especially delicious in substantial lunchtime sandwiches, but also suits open sandwiches. Use tuna in sunflower oil for a richer filling, or in brine for a lighter one.

Fills 3 rounds sandwiches

INGREDIENTS
75 g/3 oz can tuna, drained
25 g/1 oz/2 tbsp softened butter or margarine
15 ml/1 tbsp tomato ketchup
15 ml/1 tbsp mayonnaise
salt and freshly ground black pepper

Put the tuna in a bowl and flake with a fork. Add the butter or margarine, tomato ketchup and mayonnaise and season to taste. Mix well until blended.

Egg & Cress Filling

Curd cheese gives this filling a smooth and creamy base that is not too rich. Egg & Cress is a tasty filling to use just as it is, or use it as a base for open sandwiches topped with good-quality ham or thinly sliced, crunchy red peppers and olives.

Fills 3 rounds sandwiches

INGREDIENTS
2 hard-boiled eggs, shelled and
    finely chopped
50 g/2 oz/¼ cup curd cheese
30 ml/2 tbsp mayonnaise
1 carton mustard and cress
salt and freshly ground black pepper

Mix the ingredients together in a bowl until thoroughly combined and smooth, and season to taste.

11

Elegant Egg Sandwiches

A well–made egg sandwich is one of the best and quickest snacks. Here are two favourite fillings.

Serves 6

INGREDIENTS
12 thin slices white or brown bread
50 g/2oz/¼ cup softened butter
slices of lemon, to garnish

FOR THE EGG AND CRESS FILLING
2 small hard-boiled eggs, finely chopped
30 ml/2 tbsp mayonnaise
½ punnet mustard and cress
salt and freshly ground
   black pepper

FOR THE EGG AND TUNA FILLING
2 small hard-boiled eggs, finely chopped
25 g/1 oz canned tuna in oil, drained
   and mashed
5 ml/1 tsp paprika
squeeze of lemon juice
25 g/1 oz piece cucumber, peeled and
   thinly sliced

2 To make the egg and cress filling, mix the chopped eggs with the mayonnaise, cress and seasoning. Layer between six slices of bread. Press down gently and cut into neat triangles.

VARIATION: For harlequin sandwiches, use a combination of white and brown bread. Use a slice of brown bread for one side of each sandwich and a slice of white for the other. Arrange them on a plate, turning the sandwiches to show alternate brown and white slices.

COOK'S TIP: These sandwiches will keep well for 2–3 hours. Cover with damp kitchen paper, then cover tightly in clear film. Chill until required.

1 Carefully trim the crusts off the bread, using a sharp knife, then spread the bread thinly with soft butter.

3 To make the egg and tuna filling, mix the chopped eggs with the tuna, paprika, lemon juice and seasoning. Put cucumber on three slices of bread, top with the tuna mixture and the rest of the bread. Press down lightly and cut each sandwich into three neat fingers.

4 Arrange all the sandwiches on a plate and garnish with lemon slices.

Cucumber Sandwiches

These traditional afternoon-tea sandwiches are easy to prepare and always popular. The cucumber slices need 30 minutes to marinate.

Makes 4

INGREDIENTS
½ cucumber
30 ml/2 tbsp white wine vinegar
50 g/2 oz/¼ cup softened butter
8 slices white bread
salt and freshly ground black pepper
cucumber butterflies, to garnish

1 Cut a few thin slices of cucumber to use as a garnish and set aside, then peel the rest and slice thinly. Place in a bowl, pour over the vinegar and set aside to marinate for 30 minutes. Drain well.

2 Butter the bread, and arrange the slices of cucumber over half the bread slices.

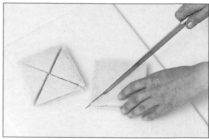

3 Sprinkle the cucumber slices with salt and pepper to taste. Cover with the remaining buttered bread to make four sandwiches. Press together firmly and cut off the crusts. Cut each sandwich into four triangles. Arrange the sandwiches fanned out attractively on a serving plate and serve garnished with the cucumber butterflies.

Bagels & Lox

Introduced from Germany into the United States with the first Jewish immigrants, bagels are now popular everywhere.

Makes 2

INGREDIENTS

2 bagels
115 g/4 oz/½ cup cream cheese
5 ml/1 tsp lemon juice
15 ml/1 tbsp chopped fresh chives
a little milk (optional)
115 g/4 oz smoked salmon
salt and freshly ground black pepper
lemon slices and dill sprigs, to garnish

1 Preheat the oven to 180°C/350°F/ Gas 4. Wrap the bagels in foil and warm them through in the oven for 10 minutes. Mix the cream cheese with the lemon juice, chives and a little milk to thin if necessary. Season to taste with salt and pepper.

2 Cut the bagels in half horizontally and spread each of the bases with half the cream cheese.

3 Arrange the smoked salmon over the cream cheese and replace the tops of the bagels.

4 Serve the bagels garnished with lemon slices and sprigs of dill.

Classic BLT

This delicious American sandwich is made with crispy fried bacon, lettuce and tomato. Choose the bread you prefer and toast it if you like.

Makes 2

INGREDIENTS
4 slices Granary bread
15 g/½ oz/1 tbsp softened butter
few crisp cos or iceberg lettuce leaves
1 large tomato, sliced
8 rashers streaky bacon
30 ml/2 tbsp mayonnaise

1 Spread two of the slices of bread with butter. Lay the lettuce over the bread and cover with sliced tomato.

2 Grill the bacon rashers until they begin to crisp, then arrange them over the sliced tomato.

3 Quickly spread the two remaining slices of bread with mayonnaise. Lay the bread over the bacon, press the sandwiches together gently and cut in half. Serve immediately.

Pastrami on Rye

Wood-smoked brisket of beef that has first been dry-cured in a mixture of garlic, sugar, salt and spices is known as pastrami.

Makes 2

INGREDIENTS
25 g/1 oz/2 tbsp softened butter
4 thin slices rye bread
15 ml/1 tbsp German mustard
115 g/4 oz wafer-thin pastrami
4 gherkins, sliced lengthways
radish chrysanthemums and spring onion
    tassels, to garnish

1 Butter the bread and spread two of the slices with a little mustard.

2 Arrange the wafer-thin pastrami slices over the mustard.

3 Top with slices of gherkin, cover with the remaining bread and press together firmly. Toast on both sides under a preheated grill until the bread turns golden brown. Serve garnished with radish chrysanthemums and spring onion tassels.

Club Sandwich

Triple-deckers, or club sandwiches, are made with three layers of bread and should be very generously filled.

Makes 1

INGREDIENTS
25 g/1 oz/2 tbsp softened butter
2 slices brown bread
1 slice white bread
2 slices rare roast beef
5 ml/1 tsp horseradish relish
  (see Cook's Tip)
few frisée lettuce leaves
1 tomato, sliced
½ avocado, peeled and sliced
30 ml/2 tbsp mayonnaise
carrot curls and stuffed olives,
  to garnish

1 Butter the slices of brown bread on one side only and the white bread on both sides.

2 Cover one of the slices of brown bread with the sliced, rare roast beef, some horseradish relish and then some frisée lettuce.

3 Cover this layer with the white bread and then arrange tomato and avocado slices on top.

4 Spread mayonnaise over the top, and sandwich with the remaining slice of brown bread.

5 Press the sandwich together lightly and cut into quarters.

COOK'S TIP: To make horseradish relish, in a bowl mix together 45 ml/3 tbsp fromage frais, 20 ml/4 tsp wholegrain mustard and 20 ml/4 tsp horseradish sauce.

6 Put carrot curls and stuffed olives on to cocktail sticks and push into each sandwich to garnish.

VARIATION: If you like, try chicken with cranberry sauce or cheese with tomato chutney instead of the beef and horseradish.

Farmer's Brunch

A traditional, wholesome sandwich. Use very fresh, crusty white bread and top the cheese with a home-made chutney or relish.

Makes 2

INGREDIENTS

25 g/1 oz/2 tbsp softened butter
4 slices crusty white bread
115 g/4 oz Red Leicester or Wensleydale
   cheese, sliced
45 ml/3 tbsp chutney or relish
spring onions, or pickled onions, and tomato
   wedges, to serve

1 Spread the softened butter over one side of each slice of white bread. Cover two slices of the bread with the Red Leicester or Wensleydale cheese slices.

2 Spread chutney or relish over the remaining two slices and place them over the cheese.

3 Cut each sandwich in half and serve with spring onions or pickled onions, and tomato wedges.

Crab & Avocado Sandwich

The flavours of crab and avocado combine together very successfully to make this most delicious sandwich.

Makes 4

INGREDIENTS
175 g/6 oz canned crab meat
   in brine, drained
2 spring onions, chopped
120 ml/4 fl oz/½ cup mayonnaise
1 large avocado, peeled, halved and stoned
15 ml/1 tbsp lemon juice
50 g/2 oz/¼ cup softened butter
8 slices Granary bread
salt and freshly ground black pepper
frisée leaves, to garnish

1 Mix the crab meat with the spring onions, seasoning and 30 ml/2 tbsp of the mayonnaise.

2 Cut the peeled avocado halves into thin slices and immediately brush with lemon juice to prevent them discoloring.

3 Butter the bread and divide the crab meat among four of the slices, spreading it to the edges.

4 Cover the crab meat with slices of avocado. Spread the remaining mayonnaise over the top. Cover with the remaining bread slices and press together firmly. Cut off the crusts and cut the sandwiches diagonally into quarters. Serve the sandwiches garnished with frisée leaves.

Prawn, Tomato & Mayonnaise Sandwich

A garlicky tomato mayonnaise complements the prawns wonderfully in this sandwich. Add an elegant finishing touch with a garnish of fresh herbs, such as marjoram or parsley.

Makes 2

INGREDIENTS
25 g/1 oz/2 tbsp softened butter
5 ml/1 tsp sun-dried tomato paste
4 slices wholemeal bread
1 bunch watercress, trimmed
45 ml/3 tbsp tomato mayonnaise
  (see Cook's Tip)
115 g/4 oz/1 cup frozen cooked peeled
  prawns, thawed and patted dry

1 Mix the butter and sun-dried tomato paste together until well blended.

2 Spread on the bread, then arrange watercress on two of the slices.

3 Spread tomato mayonnaise to the edges, then divide the prawns equally among the bread slices, on top of the watercress. Sandwich together with the remaining bread slices and cut in half or quarters.

COOK'S TIP: To make tomato mayonnaise, peel, seed and roughly chop 1 tomato and place in a blender with 1 small crushed garlic clove, 5 ml/1 tsp soft brown sugar and 10 ml/2 tsp tomato purée. Process until smooth and stir into 120 ml/4 fl oz/½ cup mayonnaise. Store in the fridge until needed.

22

Chicken & Curry Mayonnaise Sandwich

This tasty snack is a very useful and appetizing way of using leftover pieces of chicken.

Makes 2

INGREDIENTS
4 slices Granary bread
25 g/1 oz/2 tbsp softened butter
115 g/4 oz cooked chicken without
   skin, sliced
45 ml/3 tbsp curry mayonnaise
   (see Cook's Tip)
1 bunch watercress, trimmed

1 Spread the Granary bread evenly with butter and arrange the chicken over two of the slices.

2 Spread curry mayonnaise over the chicken slices.

3 Arrange sprigs of watercress on top, leaving some for a garnish, cover with the remaining bread and cut in half.

COOK'S TIP: To make curry mayonnaise, mix together 120 ml/ 4 fl oz/½ cup mayonnaise, 120 ml/ 4 fl oz/½ cup concentrated curry sauce, 2.5 ml/½ tsp lemon juice and 10 ml/2 tsp sieved apricot jam.

Welsh Rarebit

Popularly called Welsh Rabbit, this snack is an old favourite.

Serves 2

INGREDIENTS
2 thick slices white bread
15 g/½ oz/1 tbsp softened butter
100 g/3¾ oz Cheddar or similar cheese, sliced
10 ml/2 tsp spicy or mild mustard or good pinch of paprika or cayenne pepper
freshly ground black pepper
tomato quarters and basil, to garnish

1 Preheat the grill and lightly toast the bread on both sides. Spread sparingly with butter, then top with the cheese, leaving a narrow border around the edges. Heat under the grill until the cheese melts and starts to brown.

2 Spread the cheese quickly with some mustard or sprinkle with a little paprika or cayenne. Add a grinding of pepper. Cut in half and serve garnished with tomato and basil.

Croque-monsieur

This tasty French snack means "gentleman's crunch".

Serves 2

INGREDIENTS
15 g/½ oz/1 tbsp softened butter
4 thin slices country-style bread
75 g/3 oz Gruyère or Cheddar cheese, sliced
2 lean honey roast ham slices
freshly ground black pepper
flat leaf parsley, to garnish

1 Preheat a sandwich toaster or the grill. Lightly butter the bread and lay the cheese and ham on two of the slices. Season with pepper. Top with the other slices of bread and press together.

2 Cook in the sandwich toaster, following the manufacturer's instructions, or grill until browned on both sides. Garnish with parsley.

Right: Welsh Rarebit (top); Croque-monsieur.

Tuna Melt

Melts can also be made with a variety of meats, such as salami, pastrami or chicken, then covered with cheese and grilled.

Makes 2

INGREDIENTS
90 g/3½ oz can tuna, drained and flaked
30 ml/2 tbsp mayonnaise
15 ml/1 tbsp finely chopped celery
15 ml/1 tbsp finely chopped
    spring onion
15 ml/1 tbsp chopped fresh parsley
5 ml/1 tsp lemon juice
25 g/1 oz/2 tbsp softened butter
4 slices wholemeal bread
50 g/2 oz Gruyère or Emmenthal
    cheese, sliced
celery leaves and radish roses,
    to garnish

1 Mix together the tuna, mayonnaise, celery, spring onion, parsley and lemon juice in a small bowl.

2 Butter the bread with half the butter and spread the tuna filling over two slices. Cover with the cheese, then sandwich with the remaining bread.

3 Butter the top of the bread and place under a moderate grill for 1–2 minutes. Turn over, spread with butter and grill for a further 1–2 minutes until the cheese begins to melt. Garnish with celery and radish.

Reuben Sandwich

This New York Jewish creation combines rye bread or pumpernickel, salt beef, Gruyère cheese and sauerkraut.

Makes 2

INGREDIENTS
25 g/1 oz/2 tbsp softened butter
4 slices rye bread or pumpernickel
50 g/2 oz wafer-thin salt beef
50 g/2 oz Gruyère or Emmenthal
   cheese, sliced
15 ml/1 tbsp tomato ketchup
30 ml/2 tbsp mayonnaise
90 ml/6 tbsp sauerkraut
sliced gherkins and celery leaves,
   to garnish

1 Preheat the grill. Butter the rye bread or pumpernickel and place salt beef on two of the slices. Arrange cheese on the other slices.

2 Mix the tomato ketchup and mayonnaise with the sauerkraut.

3 Pile the sauerkraut mixture on top of the cheese and spread to the edges.

4 Lay the other bread slices, beef-side down, on top of the sauerkraut. Butter the bread on top, then grill for 1–2 minutes until crisp. Turn over, butter the second side and grill for a further 1–2 minutes until the cheese just begins to melt. Serve garnished with gherkin slices and celery leaves.

VARIATION: Replace the salt beef with pastrami.

Fried Mozzarella Sandwich

When making these tasty Italian snacks, try to find buffalo milk mozzarella for the best flavour.

Makes 2

INGREDIENTS
115 g/4 oz mozzarella cheese, thickly sliced
4 thick slices white bread
1 egg
30 ml/2 tbsp milk
vegetable oil, for frying
salt and freshly ground black pepper
tomato rose and basil, to garnish

1 Lay the cheese on two slices of bread and season to taste. Top with the remaining bread slices, pressing firmly together, to make two cheese sandwiches. Cut in half diagonally, if wished.

2 Beat the egg with the milk. Season with salt and pepper to taste and pour into a shallow dish.

3 Carefully dip the sandwiches into the egg and milk mixture until thoroughly coated. Leave to soak while heating the oil in a large, heavy frying pan.

4 Fry the sandwiches, in batches if necessary, until golden brown and crisp on both sides. Remove from the frying pan and drain well on kitchen paper. Garnish with a tomato rose and basil sprig, and serve immediately.

Crispy Hot Dogs

Succulent frankfurters are enclosed in crisp little envelopes – use grilled chipolata sausages if you prefer, and vary the flavouring with different sauces.

Makes 8

INGREDIENTS
8 slices white or brown bread,
  crusts removed
50 g/2 oz/¼ cup softened butter
15 ml/1 tbsp German mustard
8 frankfurters
sauerkraut, to serve
tomato wedges and flat leaf parsley,
  to garnish

1 Preheat the oven to 200°C/400°F/ Gas 6. Roll the bread slices lightly with a rolling pin so that they roll up more easily.

2 Spread the bread with a little butter and mustard.

3 Place a frankfurter diagonally across each slice of bread and roll up tightly, securing with a cocktail stick. Spread each roll with butter and place on a baking sheet. Bake for 15–20 minutes, or until golden. Meanwhile, heat the sauerkraut. Remove the cocktail sticks from the hot dogs and serve with hot sauerkraut and a garnish of tomato wedges and flat leaf parsley.

Filled Croissants

Croissants are versatile and can be used with sweet or savoury fillings. Smoked salmon with egg, or stilton and pear, are two options.

Makes 2

INGREDIENTS
2 croissants
knob of butter
2 eggs
15 ml/1 tbsp double cream
50 g/2 oz smoked salmon, chopped
salt and freshly ground
    black pepper
1 fresh dill sprig and chive flowers,
    to garnish

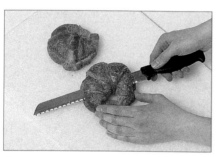

1 Preheat the oven to 180°C/350°F/ Gas 4. Slice the croissants in half horizontally and warm in the oven for 5–6 minutes.

VARIATION: Soften 115 g/4 oz Stilton cheese with a fork and mix in 1 peeled, cored and chopped ripe pear and 15 ml/1 tbsp chopped fresh chives with a little black pepper. Spoon into a split croissant and bake in a preheated oven for 5 minutes.

2 Melt a knob of butter in a small pan. Beat the eggs in a bowl with seasoning to taste.

3 Add the eggs to the pan and cook for 2 minutes, stirring constantly until lightly scrambled. Remove from the heat and stir in the double cream and chopped smoked salmon.

4 Spoon the smoked salmon and egg mixture into the warmed croissants and serve immediately, garnished with the dill sprig and chive flowers.

Köfte in Pitta Pockets

Turkish meatballs, or köfte, are made with minced lamb and flavoured with cumin and mint. They are delicious tucked into pitta bread.

Makes 4

INGREDIENTS
1 slice bread
225 g/8 oz minced lamb
1 garlic clove, crushed
1 small onion, finely chopped
5 ml/1 tsp ground cumin
15 ml/1 tbsp chopped fresh mint
15 ml/1 tbsp pine nuts
flour, for coating
vegetable oil, for frying
4 pitta breads
1 onion, cut into thin rings
2 tomatoes, sliced or cut
  into wedges
salt and freshly ground
  black pepper
fresh mint sprigs, to garnish
ready-made Tzatziki, to serve

1 Preheat the oven to 220°C/425°F/ Gas 7. Soak the bread in water for 5 minutes, then squeeze dry and add to the next six ingredients with seasoning. Mix well, then shape into small balls the size of a walnut, using dampened hands so that the mixture does not stick. Coat in flour.

2 Heat the oil in a frying pan and fry the meatballs for about 6 minutes, turning frequently, until golden brown.

3 Heat the pitta breads in the oven for a few minutes until puffed up, then cut a thin strip off one side of each pitta to make a pocket. Fill the pittas with the meatballs, onion rings and tomato slices or wedges, garnish with mint and serve immediately with tzatziki.

Bacon, Egg & Chanterelle Sandwiches

When mid-morning hunger strikes, few mushroom lovers can resist a plate of egg and bacon sandwiches stuffed with chanterelles.

Makes 4

INGREDIENTS
350 g/12 oz unsmoked bacon
50 g/2 oz/¼ cup unsalted butter, plus extra
  for spreading
115 g/4 oz chanterelle mushrooms, trimmed
  and halved
60 ml/4 tbsp groundnut oil
4 eggs
4 large baps, split
salt and freshly ground black pepper

1 Place the bacon in a large non-stick frying pan and fry in its own fat until crisp. Transfer to a plate, cover and keep warm.

2 Melt 25 g/1 oz/2 tbsp of the butter in the pan, add the chanterelles and fry gently until soft without letting them colour. Transfer to a plate, cover and keep warm.

3 Melt the remaining butter, add the oil and heat to a moderate temperature. Break the eggs into the pan and fry as you like them – fried on only one side, or fried on both sides.

4 Toast the baps, spread with butter, then layer with bacon, chanterelles and a fried egg. Season to taste with salt and pepper, top with the second half of the bap and serve.

Ciabatta Sandwich

If you can find ciabatta bread flavoured with sun-dried tomatoes, it improves the flavour of the sandwich.

Makes 3

INGREDIENTS
60 ml/4 tbsp mayonnaise
30 ml/2 tbsp home-made or
    ready-made pesto
1 ciabatta loaf
115 g/4 oz provolone or mozzarella
    cheese, sliced
75 g/3 oz Parma ham,
    cut into strips
4 plum tomatoes, sliced
fresh basil leaves, torn
    into pieces
basil sprigs, to garnish

1 Put the mayonnaise and pesto into a small bowl and stir until thoroughly mixed together.

2 Cut the ciabatta in half horizontally and spread the cut side of both halves with the pesto mayonnaise. Lay the cheese over one half of the ciabatta.

3 Arrange the Parma ham strips over the top. Cover with the sliced tomatoes and torn basil leaves. Sandwich together with the other half and cut into three pieces. Garnish with basil and serve.

Salami Hero

This American speciality varies regionally, and can contain tuna, egg, cheese, coleslaw, salads, meats or salamis according to your taste.

Makes 2

INGREDIENTS
2 long crusty rolls
25 g/1 oz/2 tbsp softened butter
few lollo rosso lettuce or
   radicchio leaves
75 g/3 oz coleslaw
75 g/3 oz Italian salami, sliced
1 tomato, sliced
30 ml/2 tbsp mayonnaise

1 Cut the crusty rolls horizontally three-quarters of the way through, open them out sufficiently to take the filling and then butter both cut sides of each roll.

2 Arrange lollo rosso lettuce or radicchio leaves on the base, then add a spoonful of coleslaw.

3 Fold the salami slices in half and arrange over the top. Cover with more lettuce, the tomato slices and a little mayonnaise.

Omelette Roll

An unusual way to serve an omelette, but one that works extremely well.
Flavoured rolls add an extra-special touch.

Makes 4

INGREDIENTS
4 flavoured rolls, such as
    cheese and tomato
45 ml/3 tbsp crushed
    sun-dried tomatoes
8 eggs
bunch of fresh chives, chopped
60 ml/4 tbsp chopped
    sun-dried tomatoes
50 g/2 oz/¼ cup butter
small bunch of watercress
salt and freshly ground
    black pepper

1 Slice the rolls horizontally and
scoop out some of the crumb to make
a hollow. Spread the crushed sun-dried
tomatoes over the bread.

2 Break the eggs into a bowl, add
60 ml/4 tbsp water, the chives and
chopped sun-dried tomatoes and
season to taste with salt and pepper.
Whisk well with a fork.

3 Melt one-quarter of the butter in a
small omelette pan. Ladle in about
one-quarter of the egg mixture, then, as
it begins to set, draw the sides towards
the middle using a palette knife, so
that more egg touches the hot pan.
Repeat a couple of times.

4 When the egg is just set, lift the
edge of the omelette nearest the
handle, tilting the pan away from you.

5 Flip the omelette over and gently
slip it in to one roll. Repeat to make
three more omelette rolls in the same
way. Tuck some watercress under the
omelettes and serve immediately.

Oriental Chicken Sandwich

This filling is also good served in warmed pitta bread, in which case cut the chicken into small cubes before marinating. Grill on skewers.

Makes 2

INGREDIENTS
15 ml/1 tbsp soy sauce
5 ml/1 tsp clear honey
5 ml/1 tsp sesame oil
1 garlic clove, crushed
175 g/6 oz skinless boneless chicken
  breast portion
4 slices white bread
25 g/1 oz/¼ cup beansprouts
25 g/1 oz/¼ cup seeded and finely sliced
  red pepper
2 fresh parsley sprigs, to garnish

FOR THE PEANUT SAUCE
7.5 ml/1½ tsp sunflower oil
½ small onion, chopped
1 garlic clove, crushed
2. 5ml/½ tsp ground cumin
2.5 ml/½ tsp ground coriander
1.5 ml/¼ tsp chilli powder
22.5 ml/4½ tsp crunchy peanut butter
about 30 ml/2 tbsp water
5 ml/1 tsp soy sauce
2.5 ml/½ tsp lemon juice

1 First make the peanut sauce. Heat the oil in a small pan and fry the onion until softened. Add the garlic and spices and fry, stirring constantly, for 1 further minute. Stir in the peanut butter and blend in the water. Bring to the boil, stirring constantly, cover and simmer for 5 minutes.

2 Turn into a bowl and stir in the soy sauce and lemon juice. Thin with a little more water if you like. Set aside until required.

3 Preheat the grill. Mix together the soy sauce, honey, sesame oil and garlic in a small bowl. Brush over the chicken portion. Grill the chicken for 3–4 minutes on each side until cooked through, then slice thinly.

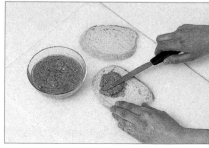

4 Spread two slices of the bread with some of the peanut sauce. Lay the chicken slices on the sauce-covered bread, then spread a little more sauce over the chicken.

5 Sprinkle over the beansprouts and red pepper and sandwich together with the remaining slices of bread. Serve, garnished with parsley. Store the remaining peanut sauce in a covered container in the fridge for up to 3 days.

Fontina Pan Bagna

When the weather is hot, a crusty flute or baguette filled with juicy tomatoes, crisp red onion, green pepper, thinly sliced Fontina and sliced black olives makes a refreshing snack.

Serves 2–4

INGREDIENTS
1 small red onion, thinly sliced
1 fresh flute or baguette
extra virgin olive oil
3 ripe plum tomatoes, thinly sliced
1 small green pepper, halved, seeded and
    thinly sliced
200 g/7 oz Fontina cheese,
    thinly sliced
about 12 stoned black olives, sliced
a handful of flat leaf parsley or
    basil leaves
salt and freshly ground black pepper

3 Top with the pepper slices, followed by the onion slices, then add the cheese and olives. Sprinkle over the parsley or basil leaves and season again.

4 Press the halves together, then wrap tightly in clear film to compress. Chill for at least 1 hour. Unwrap and cut diagonally in thick slices to serve.

1 Soak the red onion in plenty of cold water for at least an hour, then drain well in a colander, tip on to kitchen paper and pat dry.

2 Slice the flute or baguette in half lengthways and brush the cut sides well with olive oil. Lay the tomato slices down one side and season well.

COOK'S TIP: Fontina is a delicately flavoured Italian alpine cheese made from unpasteurized cow's milk. You could also try Taleggio, another Italian cheese, or Havarti from Denmark.

Yacht Sandwich

This cheerful yacht will delight any child. The basic sandwich shape is quick to make; add the trimmings if you have time.

Makes 1

INGREDIENTS
1 sandwich round made with
    chosen filling
butter
chopped fresh parsley
few pretzel sticks
mild paprika
shredded lettuce
tomato ketchup and small pieces of
    lemon rind and cucumber,
    to garnish (optional)

1 Remove the crusts from the sandwich and cut two triangular sails from it. Shape the remaining piece of sandwich to resemble a boat.

2 Spread the long edges of the sails with a little butter and dip into the chopped parsley.

3 Turn one sail over and arrange two sides together with the pretzel sticks in the centre to represent the mast.

4 Spread the boat shape with a little butter, dip into paprika and position below the sails. Arrange shredded lettuce underneath to represent the waves of the sea. If you like, you can pipe a number on the sail with tomato ketchup. To complete the boat you could also cut out a sun from lemon rind and a flag from a piece of cucumber.

Sailing Ships

A novelty sandwich that you can prepare with different fillings. The processed cheese slices make wonderful sails.

Makes 12

INGREDIENTS
6 bridge rolls
225 g/8 oz chosen filling
2 tomatoes, quartered and seeded
chopped fresh parsley (optional)
2 radishes
6 processed cheese slices

1 Cut each roll in half horizontally and trim the base so that it stands evenly. Put 15 ml/1 tbsp of the filling on to each half and spread to the edges, doming it slightly. Cut the tomatoes into thin strips and arrange around the edge of each half-roll.

2 Surround the filling with a border of chopped parsley, if you like.

3 Cut the radishes into strips and two triangles. Cut the cheese into triangles. Thread each sail on to a cocktail stick and stand in the filling, supporting it with radish strips. Add the radish flags.

Log Cabin

This takes a little time to prepare, but is a great favourite with children.

Makes 1

INGREDIENTS
4 sandwich rounds made with chosen filling,
    crusts removed
pretzel sticks
50 g/2 oz/¼ cup curd cheese
1 tomato
1 carrot
1 radish
2.5 cm/1 in piece cucumber

1 Place two of the sandwich rounds on a board and cut each into small rectangular sandwiches. Cut each of the remaining two sandwich rounds into four triangles each.

2 Stack the rectangular sandwiches together to form the cabin and place six of the triangles on top to form the roof. (The remaining triangles can be served separately.)

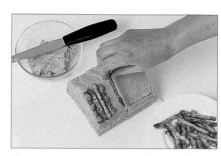

3 Arrange pretzel sticks on the roof to look like logs, sticking with a little sandwich filling or curd cheese.

4 Break some more pretzel sticks into 2.5 cm/1 in lengths and use to make a fence around the cabin, sticking in position with curd cheese.

5 Cut the tomato to make a door and windows, and the carrot to make a chimney; attach it using curd cheese and add some curd cheese smoke.

6 Cut flowers from radishes and carrot. Dice the cucumber finely and arrange on the board to resemble a winding path.

Sandwich Train

This is a simple but delightful way to make sandwiches appeal to small children, for a special occasion.

Makes 2 trains

INGREDIENTS
2 sandwich rounds made with
   soft filling
½ cucumber
radishes
a little sandwich filling
1 carrot
1 celery stick
1 cooked beetroot
cream cheese, lettuce and pretzel stick,
   to garnish (optional)

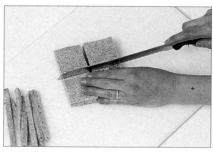

1 Remove the crusts from the sandwiches and cut each one into four squares. Cut the squares in half again to make eight small sandwiches.

COOK'S TIP: You may like to use this peanut filling for the train. Mix together 45 ml/3 tbsp crunchy peanut butter and 45 ml/3 tbsp tomato chutney. It will keep for several days in the fridge. ·

2 Make an engine using three of the sandwiches. Arrange the remaining sandwiches behind the engine. Make railway tracks from thin strips of cucumber skin.

3 Slice some radishes and stick on to the sides of the train with a little sandwich filling to resemble wheels.

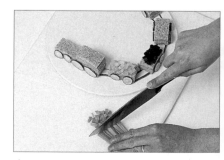

4 Cut a short length of carrot to make a funnel, and dice the remaining carrot, celery and beetroot. Pile the vegetables on to the trucks to resemble cargo.

5 Attach the carrot funnel, top with cream cheese "smoke", if you like, and place on the engine with half a radish, and a length of cucumber to make a roof for the engine. If you want to make a tree, tie some lettuce on to a pretzel stick and stick it in the centre of the plate with a small blob of cream cheese.

Wigwams

Choose a square-shaped loaf, either brown or white, so that you can cut even-size triangles; the bread should be thinly sliced.

Makes 4

INGREDIENTS
4 rounds sandwiches made with
    chosen filling
40 g/1½ oz/3 tbsp butter
chopped fresh parsley
mustard and cress, or flat leaf parsley
shredded lettuce
1 red pepper (optional)
pretzel sticks (optional)

2 Lightly butter both of the long sides of the sandwich triangles and dip in chopped parsley.

1 Cut each sandwich into triangles. Cut a slanting slice from the base of each triangle so that the sandwich will stand at an angle.

COOK'S TIP: Use whatever is your child's favourite sandwich filling, or try Iroquois pâté. Drain 2 x 130 g/ 4½ oz cans of sardines, split open the fish and remove the backbones. Mash with 225 g/8 oz/1 cup curd cheese, 15 ml/1 tbsp lemon juice and 15 ml/1 tbsp tomato ketchup.

3 Place four triangles together to form a wigwam shape. Arrange a small bunch of mustard and cress, or flat leaf parsley, to fit in-between the sandwich wigwam at the top.

4 Arrange shredded lettuce around the base of the wigwam and, if you like, strips of red pepper cut zigzag fashion along one edge. Pretzel sticks may be added to represent poles.

Herring & Apple on Rye

You can use rollmops, herrings in wine sauce or any other pickled
herrings you like for this flavoursome snack.

Makes 4

INGREDIENTS
25 g/1 oz/2 tbsp softened butter
4 slices rye bread
few lettuce leaves
4 pickled herring fillets
1 red apple, cored and sliced
5 ml/1 tsp lemon juice
fennel sprigs, to garnish

FENNEL AND SOURED CREAM DRESSING
50 ml/2 fl oz/¼ cup soured cream
5 ml/1 tsp lemon juice
1 garlic clove, crushed
2.5 ml/½ tsp clear honey
15 ml/1 tbsp chopped fresh fennel
salt and freshly ground black pepper

1 First make the fennel and soured
cream dressing. Put the soured cream
into a bowl and stir in the lemon
juice, garlic and honey. Stir in the
chopped fennel and season to taste
with salt and pepper.

2 Spread the butter on the bread and
cover with a few lettuce leaves. Cut
the herring fillets in half and arrange
on top.

3 Brush the apple slices with lemon
juice and arrange round the herring.

4 Spoon over some fennel and soured
cream dressing and garnish with
fennel sprigs.

Ham & Asparagus Slice

Be creative in your arrangement of the ingredients here. You could make ham cornets or wrap the asparagus in the ham.

Makes 4

INGREDIENTS

12 asparagus spears
115 g/4 oz/½ cup cream cheese
4 slices rye bread
4 slices ham
few frisée lettuce leaves
30 ml/2 tbsp mayonnaise, plus extra
   to serve (optional)
4 radish roses, to garnish
salt

1 Cook the asparagus in lightly salted boiling water until tender. Drain, pat dry with kitchen paper and cool.

2 Spread cream cheese over the rye bread and arrange the ham in folds over the top.

3 Lay three asparagus spears on each sandwich. Fan them out attractively or place them between folds of ham.

4 Arrange frisée lettuce leaves on top of the asparagus spears and spoon over some mayonnaise.

5 Garnish the open sandwiches with radish roses and serve extra mayonnaise separately in a small bowl, if you like.

Smoked Salmon & Gravlax Sauce

Use gravlax – cured fresh salmon – instead of smoked salmon, if you wish. It can be bought in most supermarkets and delicatessens.

Makes 8

INGREDIENTS
25 g/1 oz/2 tbsp softened butter
5 ml/1 tsp grated lemon rind
4 slices rye or pumpernickel bread
115 g/4 oz smoked salmon
few frisée lettuce leaves
lemon slices
cucumber slices
dill sprigs, to garnish

FOR THE GRAVLAX SAUCE
15 ml/1 tbsp German mustard
2.5 ml/½ tsp caster sugar
2.5 ml/½ tsp wine vinegar
15 ml/1 tbsp vegetable oil
15 ml/1 tbsp soured cream
10 ml/2 tsp chopped fresh dill

1 First make the gravlax sauce. Beat the mustard with the sugar and vinegar. Gradually add the oil, beating well between each addition. Mix in the soured cream and dill and set aside.

2 Mix the softened butter and lemon rind together, spread over the rye bread or pumpernickel, and cut the slices in half diagonally.

3 Arrange the smoked salmon over the top to cover.

4 Add a few frisée lettuce leaves and a lemon or cucumber slice. Spoon over some gravlax sauce, then garnish with dill. Serve the remaining sauce separately, if you like.

Scrambled Egg & Tomato Fingers

Pumpernickel makes a good firm base for these finger sandwiches and its flavour combines especially well with that of scrambled egg.

Makes 6

INGREDIENTS
25 g/1 oz/2 tbsp softened butter
2 slices pumpernickel bread
2 eggs
15 ml/1 tbsp milk
15 ml/1 tbsp single cream
30 ml/2 tbsp chopped fresh chives
mustard and cress
3 canned anchovy fillets, halved
2 sun-dried tomatoes,
    cut into strips
salt and freshly ground black pepper
tomato rose and spring onion tassel,
    to garnish

1 Butter the pumpernickel and cut into six fingers.

2 Whisk the eggs lightly with the milk and add seasoning to taste. In a pan, cook the eggs in a little melted butter over a gentle heat, stirring constantly until lightly scrambled. Stir in the cream and chives, and leave to cool.

3 Arrange a little mustard and cress at the ends of the pumpernickel fingers and spoon over the egg. Place the anchovies and sun-dried tomato strips on top of the egg. Garnish with a tomato rose and spring onion tassel.

Roquefort & Pear

The traditional combination of Roquefort and pear is delicious, but other blue cheeses such as Stilton or Cambozola can be used instead.

Makes 4

INGREDIENTS
4 slices brioche loaf
115 g/4 oz/½ cup curd cheese
few rocket sprigs
115 g/4 oz Roquefort
    cheese, sliced
1 ripe pear, quartered, cored
    and sliced
juice of ½ lemon
4 pecan nuts, to garnish
viola flowers,
    to garnish (optional)

2 Arrange rocket leaves on top of the curd cheese. Place the sliced Roquefort on top.

1 Lightly toast the brioche and spread with the curd cheese.

COOK'S TIP: As the toasted brioche will become soft once it is filled, these open sandwiches must be eaten as soon as they are prepared.

3 Brush the pear slices with lemon juice to prevent discoloration. Arrange the pear slices, overlapping in a fan shape, on the cheese.

4 Garnish with pecan nuts, whole or chopped, and a viola flower if you wish. Serve immediately.

VARIATION: For a change, try apple with Cheddar, Stilton, Red Leicester, Brie or Camembert.

Celebration Sandwiches

Impressive and appetizing, open sandwiches are a good choice for lunch parties whether large or small.

Smoked Salmon with Dill

This is a simple, classic open-sandwich topping, for lunch or brunch and is always popular on a party table.

Makes 4

INGREDIENTS
4 slices light rye bread
225 g/8 oz smoked salmon,
  thinly sliced
20 ml/4 tsp soured cream
20 ml/4 tsp chopped fresh dill
fresh dill sprigs, to garnish
4 lemon slices, to serve

FOR THE PARSLEY BUTTER
50 g/2 oz/¼ cup unsalted butter, softened
15–30 ml/1–2 tbsp finely chopped
  fresh parsley

1 First make the parsley butter. Cream the butter in a small bowl and gradually beat in chopped parsley to taste.

2 Spread the rye bread with the parsley butter, and cut diagonally in half. Fold the slices of smoked salmon and arrange them, overlapping, on the bread.

3 Top each slice with a spoon of soured cream and a sprinkling of chopped dill. Serve, garnished with dill sprigs and with slices of lemon.

Smoked Mackerel

The rich flavour of smoked mackerel served with spicy horseradish is a winning combination.

Makes 4

INGREDIENTS
4 slices dark rye bread
  or pumpernickel
20 ml/4 tsp creamed horseradish
225 g/8 oz smoked mackerel fillets,
  skinned and flaked

TO GARNISH
1 tomato, peeled, seeded
  and diced
1 dill pickle or 7.5 cm/3 in piece of
  cucumber, diced
15 ml/1 tbsp very finely chopped
  onion or fresh flat leaf parsley

1 Spread the slices of bread with the creamed horseradish, and cut diagonally in half. Top with the flaked fish.

2 Just before serving, sprinkle diced tomato, diced dill pickle or cucumber and chopped onion or parsley evenly over the fish to garnish.

Above right: Italian Ham & Mango (top); Smoked Mackerel (left); Smoked Salmon with Dill.

Italian Ham & Mango

The flavour and texture of wafer-thin slices of Parma ham are perfectly complemented by juicy, fresh mango.

Makes 4

INGREDIENTS

25 g/1 oz/2 tbsp softened butter
4 slices Granary bread, crusts removed
1 small head radicchio or chicory
225 g/8 oz Parma ham, thinly sliced
1 fresh mango
8 fresh basil leaves, shredded
extra virgin olive oil, for drizzling (optional)
fresh basil sprigs, to garnish

1 Butter the Granary bread, and cut diagonally in half. Arrange a little radicchio or chicory on each piece of bread. Trim the fat from the ham and arrange it in folds on the radicchio or chicory.

2 Peel the mango and cut the flesh either side of the large, flat stone. Slice the flesh.

3 Top each sandwich with two to three mango slices and a sprinkling of shredded basil. Drizzle with a little extra virgin olive oil, if you like. Garnish with fresh basil sprigs.

Crostini with Tomato & Anchovy

Little rounds of bread are cut from a French stick and toasted or fried, then covered with a mouthwatering savoury topping.

Makes 8

INGREDIENTS
1 small French stick (to give 8 slices)
30 ml/2 tbsp olive oil
2 garlic cloves, chopped
4 tomatoes, peeled and chopped
15 ml/1 tbsp chopped
    fresh basil
15 ml/1 tbsp tomato purée
8 canned anchovy fillets, drained
12 black olives, halved and stoned
salt and freshly ground black pepper
1 fresh basil sprig, to garnish (optional)

1 Cut the loaf diagonally into 8 slices about 1 cm/½ in thick and toast until golden on both sides.

2 Heat the oil and fry the garlic and tomatoes for 4 minutes. Stir in the basil and tomato purée and season to taste with salt and pepper.

3 Spoon a little tomato mixture on to each slice of bread. Place an anchovy fillet on each one and some olives. Garnish with a basil sprig, if using. Serve.

Spicy Chicken Canapés

These tiny little cocktail sandwiches have a spicy filling, finished with different toppings. Use square bread so that you can cut more rounds.

Makes 14

INGREDIENTS
75 g/3 oz/⅓ cup finely chopped
  cooked chicken
2 spring onions, finely chopped
30 ml/2 tbsp chopped red pepper
90 ml/6 tbsp Curry Mayonnaise (see
  Classic Sandwiches)
6 slices white bread
15 ml/1 tbsp chopped fresh parsley
30 ml/2 tbsp chopped
  salted peanuts

1 Mix the chopped cooked chicken with the spring onions, red pepper and 45 ml/3 tbsp of the Curry Mayonnaise in a bowl.

2 Spread the mixture over three of the bread slices and sandwich with the remaining bread, pressing together. Spread the remaining curry mayonnaise over the top and cut into 14 x 4 cm/ 1½ in circles using a plain cutter.

3 Dip seven rounds into the parsley and seven into the nuts and serve.

Tapenade & Quail's Egg Canapés

These tasty party sandwiches are strongly flavoured with tapenade –
a purée made from capers, olives and anchovies.

Makes 8

INGREDIENTS
4 quail's eggs
1 small baguette
45 ml/3 tbsp tapenade
a few frisée lettuce leaves
3 small tomatoes, sliced and halved
2 black olives, stoned and quartered
4 canned anchovy fillets,
    halved lengthways
chopped fresh parsley, to garnish

1 Place the quail's eggs in a pan of
cold water, bring to the boil and cook
for 3 minutes. Leave to cool, then shell.

2 Cut the baguette into eight slices, on
the diagonal, and spread with tapenade.

3 Arrange a little frisée lettuce and a
half slice of tomato on top of each
piece of bread.

4 Halve the quail's eggs and place half
on top of each tomato slice.

5 Top each egg with a quartered
olive and a halved anchovy fillet, and
garnish with chopped parsley.

Asparagus Rolls

Use green asparagus as it is usually thinner and looks more attractive.
A 350 g/12 oz can usually contains about 20 spears.

Makes 20

INGREDIENTS
20 slices wholemeal bread, crusts removed
115 g/4 oz/½ cup softened butter
350 g/12 oz can asparagus tips, drained
salt and freshly ground black pepper
lemon slices and herb flowers, to garnish

1 Roll the bread lightly with a rolling pin (this makes it easier to roll up without cracking). Mix the softened butter and seasoning and spread over each slice of bread.

2 Lay an asparagus tip at one end of the bread with the tip protruding over the edge slightly.

3 Roll up the bread tightly like a Swiss roll and press the end so that the butter sticks it together.

4 Pack the rolls tightly together, wrap in clear film and chill for 1 hour so that they set in position and do not unwind when served. Serve garnished with lemon slices and herb flowers.

Sandwich Horns

Makes 9

INGREDIENTS
9 thin slices bread of your choice,
   crusts removed
115 g/4 oz/½ cup cottage cheese
15 ml/1 tbsp mixed chopped
   fresh herbs
50 g/2 oz smoked salmon pieces
75 ml/5 tbsp double cream
5 ml/1 tsp lemon juice
1 quantity Avocado Filling (see Mayonnaise
   & Simple Fillings)
salt and freshly ground black pepper
few fresh herb sprigs and lemon
   slices, to garnish

1 Cut one corner off each slice of
bread, rounding it slightly.

2 Mix the cottage cheese and chopped
herbs and season to taste. Spread three
rounds with about half of this mixture.

3 Lift the two sides and fold one over
the other with the rounded area at the
base of the horn. Stick the bread in
position with the filling. Secure with a
cocktail stick and chill for 20 minutes.
Hold the horn upright in one hand
and spoon in the remaining filling.

4 Put the smoked salmon in a
blender with the cream, lemon juice
and some pepper. Blend briefly. Use
this and the Avocado Filling to make
three horns of each. Remove the
cocktail sticks before serving and
garnish with herbs and lemon.

Striped Sandwiches

Makes 32

INGREDIENTS

6 slices brown bread
4 slices white bread
1 quantity Tuna & Tomato Filling (see
  Mayonnaise & Simple Fillings)
½ quantity Egg & Cress Filling (as above)
Cheese & Chive Filling (see Cook's Tip)
cucumber slices, fresh chives and
  fresh herb flowers, to garnish

1 Start with a slice of brown bread and spread it with Tuna & Tomato Filling.

2 Place a slice of white bread on top and spread this with some Egg & Cress Filling.

3 Repeat with Cheese & Chive Filling, then the tuna again, using brown and white bread alternately. Repeat with the remaining fillings and bread. Wrap in foil and chill for 2 hours.

4 Unwrap, cut off the crusts and, using a sharp knife, cut into 1 cm/½ in slices. Cut the slices in half and serve garnished with cucumber slices, chives and fresh herb flowers if liked.

COOK'S TIP: For the Cheese & Chive Filling, blend together 50 g/ 2 oz/¼ cup cream cheese and 45 ml/3 tbsp chopped chives.

This edition is published by Southwater

Distributed in the UK by
The Manning Partnership
251–253 London Road East
Batheaston
Bath BA1 7RL
tel. 01225 852 727
fax 01225 852 852

Distributed in Canada by
General Publishing.
895 Don Mills Road
400–402 Park Centre
Toronto, Ontario M3C 1W3
tel. 416 445 3333
fax 416 445 5991

Published in the USA by
Anness Publishing Inc.
27 West 20th Street
Suite 504
New York NY 10011
fax 212 807 6813

Distributed in Australia by
Sandstone Publishing
Unit 1, 360 Norton Street
Leichhardt
New South Wales 2040
tel. 02 9560 7888
fax 02 9560 7488

Southwater is an imprint of Anness Publishing Ltd
Hermes House, 88–89 Blackfriars Road, London SE1 8HA
tel. 020 7401 2077; fax 020 7633 9499

© Anness Publishing Limited 2001

1 3 5 7 9 10 8 6 4 2

Publisher: Joanna Lorenz
Managing Editor: Helen Sudell
Editor: Valerie Ferguson
Series Designer: Bobbie Colgate Stone
Designer: Andrew Heath
Production Controller: Joanna King
Editorial Reader: Diane Ashmore

Recipes contributed by: Janet Brinkworth,
Roz Denny, Carole Handslip, Bridget Jones,
Steven Wheeler.

Photography: Karl Adamson, Edward Allwright,
James Duncan, John Heseltine.

Printed in China

Notes:
For all recipes, quantities are given in both metric
and imperial measures and, where appropriate,
measures are also given in standard cups
and spoons. Follow one set, but not a mixture,
because they are not interchangeable.

Standard spoon and cup measures are level.

1 tsp = 5 ml   1 tbsp = 15 ml

1 cup = 250 ml/8 fl oz

Australian standard tablespoons are 20 ml.
Australian readers should use 3 tsp in place of
1 tbsp for measuring small quantities of gelatine,
cornflour, salt etc.

Medium eggs are used unless otherwise stated.